Beautiful Babies' Rooms
Inspiration and ideas from an expert

Belinda Nihill
Interior Designer

Copyright © 2016

All rights reserved. No part of this publication may be reproduced, stored in a retrieval system or transmitted in any form by any means without the prior permission of the copyright owner. Enquiries should be made to the publisher.

Every effort has been made to ensure that this book is free from error or omissions. However, the Publisher, the Author, the Editor or their respective employees or agents, shall not accept responsibility for injury, loss or damage occasioned to any person acting or refraining from action as a result of material in this book whether or not such injury, loss or damage is in any way due to any negligent act or omission, breach of duty or default on the part of the Publisher, the Author, the Editor, or their respective employees or agents.

The Author, the Publisher, the Editor and their respective employees or agents do not accept any responsibility for the actions of any person - actions which are related in any way to information containted in this book.

The moral right of the author has been asserted.

National Library of Australia Cataloguing-in-Publication entry

Author: Nihill, Belinda

Title: Beautiful Babies' Rooms

ISBN: 9780994412607

Subject: Interior Design, Childrens' Rooms, Nurseries

Dewey Number: 747.77

Images by agreement with photographers. Please see page 123 for full credits. The publisher has done its utmost to attribute the copyright holders of all the visual material used. If you nevertheless think that a copyright has been infringed, please contact the publisher.

Published by: Of The World Publishing
ACN 133 333 141
PO Box 8070
Bendigo South LPO VIC 3550

www.oftheworldbooks.com

Contents

- 7   Foreward
- 8   Feathering The Nest
- 10 Baby's Basics
- 12 Hugh's Nursery
- 20 Victoria's Nursery
- 29 Hugo's Nursery
- 36 Marley's Nursery
- 44 Leo's Nursery
- 54 Isabella's Nursery
- 60 Oscar's Nursery
- 68 Cooper's Nursery
- 76 Patricks' Nursery
- 82 Brydie's Nursery
- 88 Alec's Nursery
- 98 Charles' Nursery
- 106 Story's Nursery
- 117 Using A Designer
- 118 The Perfect Shelfie
- 120 Creating A Gallery
- 123 Photography Credits
- 124 Acknowledgements
- 125 About The Author

Foreward

A lot of people find it difficult to understand why you would spend a lot of time, energy and money on a special space for your baby. And, a lot of people find it difficult to understand why you wouldn't. After all, this is your baby's very first bedroom (after that tummy they lived in for nine months, of course) so it's nice to make it comfortable, safe and warm. On top of that, you – as a parent – are going to spend a lot of time in that room over the next few years. You are going to shhh, rock, cuddle, feed and read for days and nights that sometimes feel as though they will never end. So, in a way, you want to make it a place that is nice to hang out in.

Personally, I've always loved babies' rooms. They are simple and functional, yet can also be very beautiful. For those first few months they are calm and serene (before they start being inundated by all those toys!) and a little room filled with beautiful, teeny things gives you such hope and promise. Much like a little person does.

I first met Belinda (Bel) Nihill from Nest Design Studio back in 2009. We were bleary-eyed first time mothers and we gave birth to our eldest sons in the same hospital. At a time when it seemed strange to define yourself as 'mother' we all introduced ourselves as the career that we'd worked at leading up to those few weeks before. I was juggling magazine publishing with this new job of 'mum' and I was quite excited to hear that she had worked as an interior designer for many years prior. Part of my job was sourcing stunning babies rooms for one of my magazines, Little One Magazine, so imagine my delight when I imagined the sort of space the son of an interior designer might have!

I wasn't disappointed and Bel, who loved the task of putting together Hugh's room so much, decided to go out on her own as a freelancer – specialising in creating beautiful childrens' rooms. Over the years I have watched her business grow and seen the end result of stunning room after stunning room. Her knowledge is extensive and she's been able to use her years of experience to give many families a very special place for their littlest family member.

The thing that I believe makes Bel's rooms really stand out is how personal each one of them is. She doesn't just fill them with the latest, trendiest items (although she always ensures that each room is as fashionable as it is timeless) and she doesn't have a generic style that she slightly alters for clients. Each room is perfectly considered and ideal for the exact people who will be spending all of those hours in that magical (and sometimes not-so-magical) place.

It's wonderful to see this gorgeous compilation of beautiful baby spaces and so generous of Bel to share her tips and ideas so that everyone is able to be inspired by these sweet little spaces. I certainly hope you all enjoy them as much as I have.

Amy Doak
Writer, Editor and Publisher

Feathering the nest

Welcome! I will assume that, as you are here, you are a parent (or an expectant parent) looking to create a beautiful space for your baby. I speak with many of you every day and, if you are like most people, you are probably completely overwhelmed. You may have a favourite item or colour, but you're unsure where to go from here. Or perhaps you've gone out and purchased a big ticket item but you don't know how to make the room feel intimate and cosy. Or, like so many expectant parents, you've gone into a total freeze because it all just seems too hard. It's OK...you're not alone!

I understand that designing a space isn't simple for many people – and thankfully so, or else I'd be out of a job! There are, however, a few simple tips and tricks that I have used over the years that might be of help to you.

As well as helping to create hundreds of rooms for babies and children over the past six years, I've also had three of my own children in that time. Each one has received a very special room of their own and I've absolutely loved the process of being my own 'client'. Having three babies has also taught me a lot about what you need on a practical level for a baby. I live in a small house and space is at a premium – every spare square inch counts! I know how important it is to ensure your child's space is both practical *and* beautiful.

Each chapter in this book showcases a room that I have created for a little one. At the start of the chapter you will see what many people in the industry refer to as a 'design board'. I create one of these for each of my clients and then go into further detail about how they can then make the space come to life. I also provide clients with a room layout and provide them with a full list of recommendations, suppliers and more.

When a new client comes to me, I have them complete a detailed questionnaire to establish their likes and dislikes and also to get a feel for what they want out of the space. It is important to me that their baby's room fits in with the rest of the house as well as being a unique and special space on its own. I will discuss each room and a little about what the client was looking for or hoping for and the suggestions that I made to ensure that the brief was met.

I hope that, as well as enjoying these beautiful spaces, you find a little inspiration and a little motivation to create a gorgeous space for your own bundle of joy. After all, it's never too early to appreciate beautiful living and good design.

— Bel x

The Basics

When it comes to a baby's room, there are a few items that I recommend all rooms have if possible. Space and budget doesn't always allow for everything, but it will definitely make life easier if you have a few basic necessities.

A place to sleep

This one's fairly obvious, don't you think? Cot, cradle, bassinette, it doesn't really matter. Just be sure to remember that Australian Safety Standards are fairly strict and that vintage beds might not measure up. There are so many choices though – rectangle cots, oval cots, cots with sides that drop, cots that turn into junior beds. There are moses baskets, little bassinettes, hanging beds and hammocks. Beds on wheels and beds on stands. Beds that will join yours and beds that will grow with your baby. The list is endless! So, choose one that suits your lifestyle and also one that you just adore!

A place for changing bottoms

Just like beds, the variety of change tables are never ending. I've made use of both traditional change tables and change mats on top of a set of drawers with my children and both have their advantages and disadvantages. I think change tables are important – they will save your back (especially if you have a heavy bub!) and they are also great for added storage in a room. The best choice is one that will both fit the space, and the theme of the room.

A place for storing clothes

We aren't all lucky enough to have built in wardrobes so it's great to consider cupboards, drawers and shelves when it comes to finding a home for your baby's important things.

A place for showing off special things

Along the way we often find beautiful items, or perhaps they are gifted, and it just doesn't seem right to hide them away in a cupboard. Choosing and displaying those special pieces is definitely a bit of an artform and one way to ensure you have them showcased correctly is to make sure you have the right shelves or display units.

A place to sit and feed

This is a big one and many people underestimate the importance of a great feeding chair. I really splurged when I had my youngest baby and I really wish I had done that with baby number one! You spend a lot of time feeding and snuggling with your baby in those early months – especially in the middle of the night. Having a good quality chair to sit in (and sometimes nap in) is really a fabulous investment!

Beyond these items, it really comes down to personal style and taste...and really, the sky is the limit! Now it's time to dissect a few of my favourite rooms and understand why I made the choices I did when it came to adding that all important element to each special space - personality!

Hugh's Nursery

This room will always have a special place in my heart - it was my eldest son's room and the reason that Nest Design Studio really took off back in 2009. Although I must admit that I tend to steer away from trees-on-walls these days, I am very proud to say that this room has stood the test of time over the last half a decade or so! It will always remain one of my favourite spaces.

I didn't start work on Hugh's room until after he was born so I definitely knew that I was creating a space for a little boy. I was keen to make use of the traditional 'boy' colours of red, blue and white but it was important to me to find a blue that was soft and calm. Hugh was also born in 2009, so it was an era before the 'owl' craze that seemed to hit nurseries a few years later. I loved the idea of using birds or owls and I wanted a white tree to be the feature of the otherwise blue wall.

At the time, trees (and decals, really) were few and far between and I couldn't find exactly what I was looking for. So, instead of compromising and using a decal that didn't quite work in the space, I simply used a pencil and sketched the tree that I wanted on the wall. I then painted it with white paint and I was not only able to produce the perfect tree but it was a fraction of the price that a decal would have cost. It was a real lesson in thinking outside the square and also about being clear in exactly what I wanted.

As it happened, the tree became quite a sentimental part of the space and I was really sad when it came time to paint over that wall a few years on. I had lost a baby prior to falling pregnant with Hugh and my husband and I had nicknamed that little baby 'Apple' when he or she was still growing in my belly. I decided to place a little apple on the tree in honour of the baby we never got to know and that was something which was really special to me.

I love to incorporate element of DIY in to a space – it makes it really personal. As well as the tree, I used decorative paper to create the owl artwork on the walls. Six years on, the technology would have allowed me to do this on the computer and print up something big and beautiful but back then I had to be a little more creative. Even so, it shows what can be done if you're the sort of person who doesn't like computers and is on a tight budget! With Hugh being baby number one in our family, we did purchase quite a few things new. Cot, change table, chair - all the big ticket items were bought with a budget in mind.

Looking back, there's not a lot that I would have changed but I don't think I'd ever use a traditional change table again. Since having a dresser with a change pad on it for my other babies, I realise now that's a more practical road to take. However, if you've got the space, then go for it! Hugh's room was small – perfect for a baby in a cot, but certainly challenging now it is home to two little boys in single beds.

I am also quite sentimental and there were a number of things in the room that had been passed down. Some of the toys had once belonged to family members and the lovely dresser that we used belonged to Hugh's great grandmother. It was originally sage green – a really beautiful colour, actually – but it didn't work with what I'd planned for the rest of the space so I stripped it back and painted it white.

Creating Hugh's space was a really turning point for me. Before then, I had designed many other rooms but this was my very first nursery. There was a lot to love about Hugh's very first room but mostly I enjoyed how serene and calm it was. It was entirely appropriate for a little one's space and it really was the perfect first nursery.

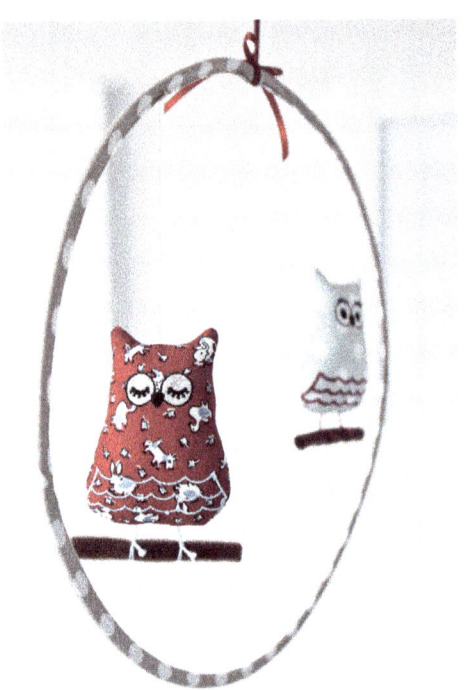

The furniture was a mix of old (the dresser once belonged to Hugh's great grandmother) and new (the cot, chair and change table were all big ticket purchases).

$\mathcal{A}$lthough the colour scheme was blue, red and white, I wasn't super strict on the tones. Having different blues (and even the addition of the green in the images) meant that as toys were added to the space they didn't look completely out of place.

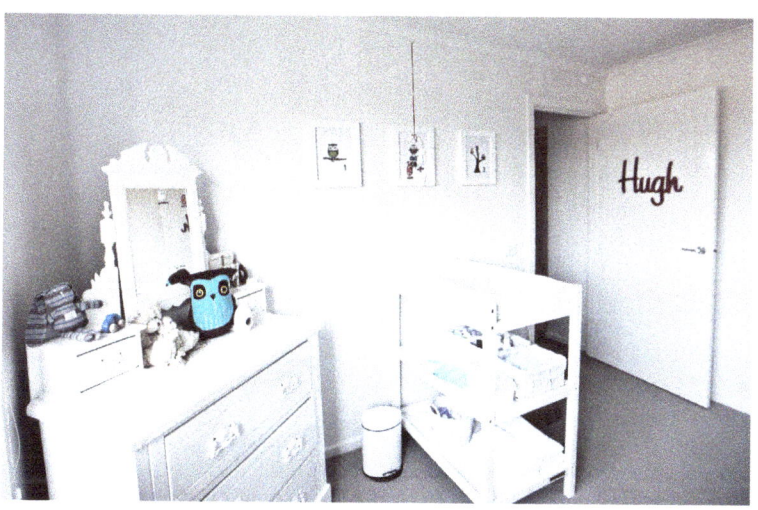

The addition of that little apple on the tree (opposite page) was in honour of the baby that we lost prior to having Hugh - we had nicknamed the baby 'Apple' and this was just a small way to honour that memory. The tree was one that I really loved and I was a little sad to paint over it when we re-did the space later.

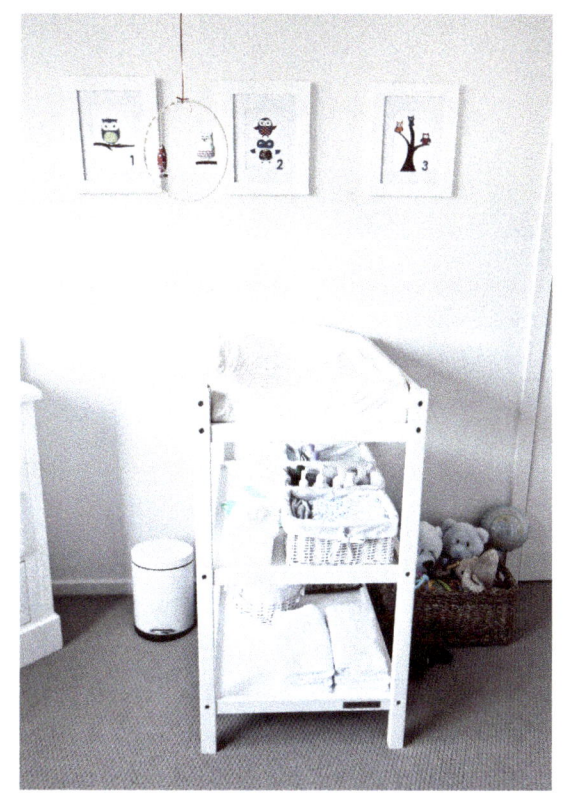

Victoria's Nursery

I initially gave Victoria's parents two options for her room - one was quite a simple, gender neutral choice and the other was very 'girlie' and heavy on the pink and the shine... and I was so thrilled when they decided to go with the glam option!

The other element that I was keen to include was a lovely gallery wall with artwork and beautiful words that inspired the family and tied the colours of the room in together.

To begin with, my clients wanted to create a gender-neutral space for their unborn child. Although they knew they were having a daughter, they hadn't let everyone know and they thought a basic design was the way to go. I presented them with a few options including this one and, in the end, they decided to go all out and run with the choice that was perhaps the most glamorous and the 'girliest'.

Victoria was their first baby and they were keen to purchase all of their items new. Although they did have a budget, buying new is definitely lots of fun as your options are then unlimited when it comes to design and style. My clients were very open to everything and their only real requirement was the addition of a 'comfortable feeding chair'. Easy fixed! Feeding chairs have come a really long way in the last few years and you can find some beautiful options these days. Nursery Works and Olli Ella (used in Victoria's room) are two of my favourite brands when it comes to custom feeding chairs that incorporate a rocker yet still look gorgeous.

The colour palette that I chose was predominantly white and pink with pops of coral, aqua and some gorgeous gold sparkly elements. The beauty of these colours is that they creates a soft and very calm feel (which is lovely for a baby's room). It also means adding bright colours along the way (which always happens once kids toys are added to the mix) isn't going to change the general vibe or feeling of the room. This was apparent soon after Victoria arrived and we took these images. The addition of toys added an extra element to the space - but it certainly didn't take away from the overall feeling of the room.

We had a few challenges with the space, the main one was that the room is an attic space and that resulted in some juggling with the floor plan to get things right. With an attic style room you have the limitation of the roofline in certain parts of the space and that can be tricky. Of course, the advantage of such a space means that you have loads of character and that adds to the overall look and feel.

In Victoria's room, the ceilings are raked and that meant that we could barely fit the change table underneath it. This also meant that we only had one wall that would accommodate a 'gallery' and that was something we wanted to include. A vent in the centre of that particular wall was another challenge however the trick there is to simply incorporate the vent into the mix. The colour and combination of frames and images meant that the vent was practically hidden from view – so the creation of the gallery actually did more than pretty up the wall!

The other space issue was the fact that the room included double doors which opened inwards, so creating a reading nook or play area behind the doors would not have been practical in the long term. However, it's important to remember that you shouldn't be put off by a challenging space. This room is divine and everything that Victoria's parents needed and wanted managed to fit in to the space we had.

My favourite part of the entire room was that magnificent wallpaper. It's a real statement piece and a lot of people are afraid of it. I think if there is ever an opportunity to experiment with colour and pattern on your walls, it's with your child's room. There is less pressure to keep it forever (just in case you don't love it to bits) and kids rooms really are meant to be a little crazy and fun.

This gorgeous rocker was a must-have for my clients. One of their key requirements was a lovely feeding chair and this one is perfect for the space. Feeding chairs aren't usually small though, so adding the perspex side table offered practicality without taking up excess space - both visually and physically.

WHAT A wonderful WORLD

Parents of girls will tell you that it's not always easy to find a pretty shade of pink - there's a lot of garish pinks out there! With Victoria's room I looked for soft, musky pinks to soften the overall scheme.

𝒥t was important for my clients that Victoria could grow in this room - it needed to be more than a baby's space. By adding this little play corner, Victoria will be encouraged very early on to start creating, crafting and enjoying tea parties with her toys!

Hugo's Nursery

It was clear in my early meetings with Hugo's mum that she was a big fan of classic Hampton's style. When we first discussed the things she loved there were two things that instantly popped into my head - some amazing wallpaper that I'd seen (which we used) and a stunning rocker (that, of course, was only sold in the USA and I had no idea how I was going to get it to Australia...but I wasn't going to let a little thing like that stop me!)

Originally, when looking at the Hamptons style brief that Hugo's mum was after, I had considered board and batten for the walls. It's a fabulous way to make a new house look 'classic' and it fit perfectly with a lot of the elements that the client had in mind for the space. We ended up (obviously!) using this brilliant wallpaper though and I am so glad. It still works with the Hamptons theme, but it's also unique and quirky enough to let the room grow as Hugo does.

I absolutely adore the wallpaper and I was so happy they were prepared to take the chance; many people see wallpaper as a risk, and I wish they didn't. Yes, it can be a messy job replacing it, but no more so than a strong coloured painted wall. This wallpaper makes a wonderful impact and I can imagine how fabulous it will look with other elements when Hugo is older.

When planning the space, we needed to work around the daybed and shelves that were being built around the window. The client knew this was something that they really wanted in the room, and they'd already started work on it when they spoke with me. The room also only has one 'full' wall, in that the other three walls also included a window, wardrobe and door. So, in order to make the pieces in the room look their best, we were a little restricted as to where everything could be placed.

The client was buying the majority of the furniture new, so this gave us plenty of flexibility. They loved this cot selection, but they were really concerned that it may not work. It is a modern shape and style and there was some doubt that it wouldn't fit well in their traditional Hamptons-esque space. However, because of the modern elements – and that wallpaper – it is the perfect fit. The grey colour sits perfectly with the grey wash of the timber pieces in the room and it really lends itself to that Ralph Lauren/preppy USA style that we wanted to achieve.

The one item that both the client and I wanted was the fabulous Nursery Works Empire Rocker feeding chair. At the time, it wasn't available in Australia but I knew it would be absolutely perfect for the space. So, I did all I could to ship it in for a reasonable price from the USA and I am so glad I did! It's absolutely gorgeous and sits beautifully in a space that is both traditional and modern.

The greatest compliment of this finished space was the fact that the client had actually used another interior designer in the past – for her daughter's room. It was quite a traditional space and the family had found it created limitations as her daughter grew. With Hugo, she didn't want to be limited and this certainly impacted almost all of my choices. Because of Hugo's room being such a great success, I was hired again...to create a new room for his big sister!

There is no doubt that the wallpaper is the strongest feature of this space, however the cot, the feeding chair and the built in unit are all solid pieces in their own right and because of this, they all work beautifully together. Other, smaller, elements would get lost in the same space.

*N*avy and white were the primary colours chosen for the space, but using creams, greys and lighter blues softens the space, as does the use of different timbers in the room.

*I*n order to create a subtle, preppy, seaside theme we added just a few touches - like the globe, the hanging shelf and the timber mirror.

Marley's Nursery

I love it when a family really puts their stamp on their new baby's room and Marley's was a great example of this. Marley's mum and dad love the beach and wanted a light and airy feel in their baby's space. Many of the real stand out pieces in this room (like the surfboard, and the oar hook) already belonged to the family and found their perfect new home in Marley's room.

𝓜arley was actually named before he was born...and with a love of surfing in mind! There is a little surf spot in Queensland called 'Little Marley's' and Marley's parents knew as soon as they were having a little boy that this would be his name. About two months before he arrived, Marley's parents contacted me about his room.

They knew they wanted something clean, light and bright; something that was classic and soothing and something that gave a little nod to the family's love of the ocean. The Dr Seuss book 'Oh The Places You Could Go' (a fabulous book for all ages!) was a favourite of the clients and the tones, colours and images in the book also offered a little inspiration. I love it when people choose something they already love to help work towards designing a space. It gives me great insight in to how their minds work and what they love (and often it's that information that tells me more about them and their tastes than the answers they give me about their design likes and dislikes!)

In Marley's case, the result was a white base with blues, yellows and grey as accent colours. The clients were keen to paint a wall, or perhaps use wallpaper and the painted stripes that we went with really ticked all of their boxes. The colour is almost a 'greige' (not quite grey, not quite beige) and because of that it offered a soft, neutral backdrop that was also modern and a little unique.

One of the great things about a colour scheme like this is that it creates a fantastic backdrop for all those toys a little boy will accumulate over time. Most boys' toys are yellow, red, blue or orange and all of these colours suit the colours we used perfectly. If Marley is fortunate to have classic wooden toys, these will also look brilliant with the scheme. By creating a soft, almost muted, scheme the client has allowed the space to evolve in a really positive way.

Already, from these images, you can see the addition of a few brightly coloured toys and books and how lovely they look in the space. In fact, if you look at page 41 and the bright primary colours of the bird mobile and how it lifts the muted tones of the oar and the pieces hanging from it, you can get an idea of how lovely this space will look and feel in the years to come.

They had already purchased the gorgeous Leander cot and change table and they had their eye on a few different chairs, but otherwise they were unsure where to go next. As the design evolved, Marley's parents were keen to add some of their own pieces to the space – such as the surfboard and the oar hook. I absolutely love it when clients do this. It makes the space so much more personal and it really gives the room a beautiful sense of warmth and purpose before their baby even arrives.

The room was a great shape and size, so I really didn't have too many challenges when working with the space, which was wonderful. Having the family so keen to make the space special was great too. The result was a unique room that suited both the family and their lifestyle perfectly.

This beach loving family was keen to incorporate elements of their lifestyle in their baby's room. The colours - yellow, white, grey and turquoise - echo the beach and details, like that gorgeous surfboard, add to the theme without it feeling overdone.

$\mathcal{A}$long with the bright yellow and turquoise, we added neutral, natural tones, like beige and brown.

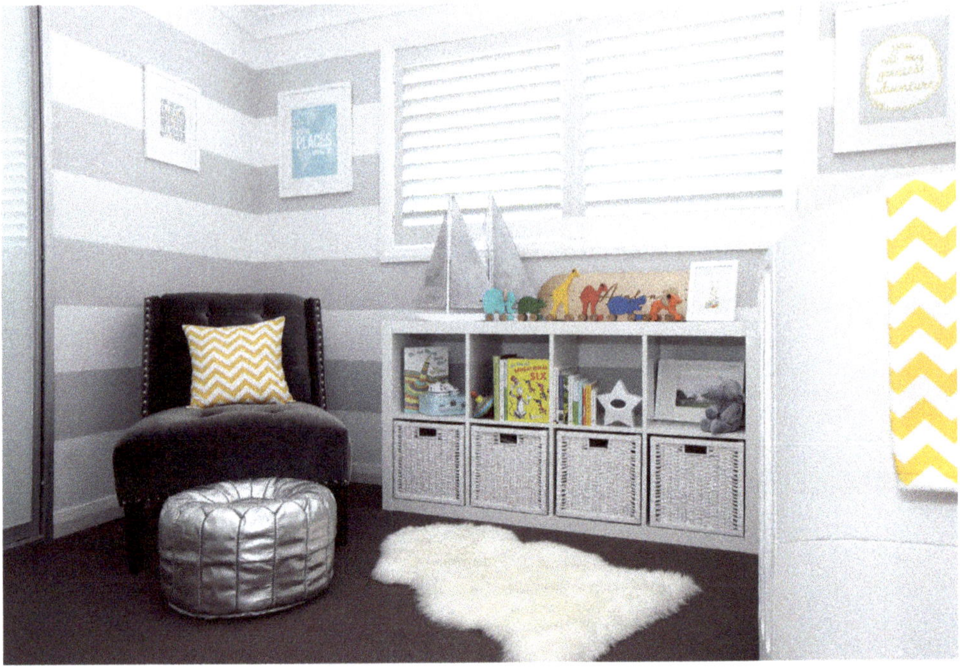

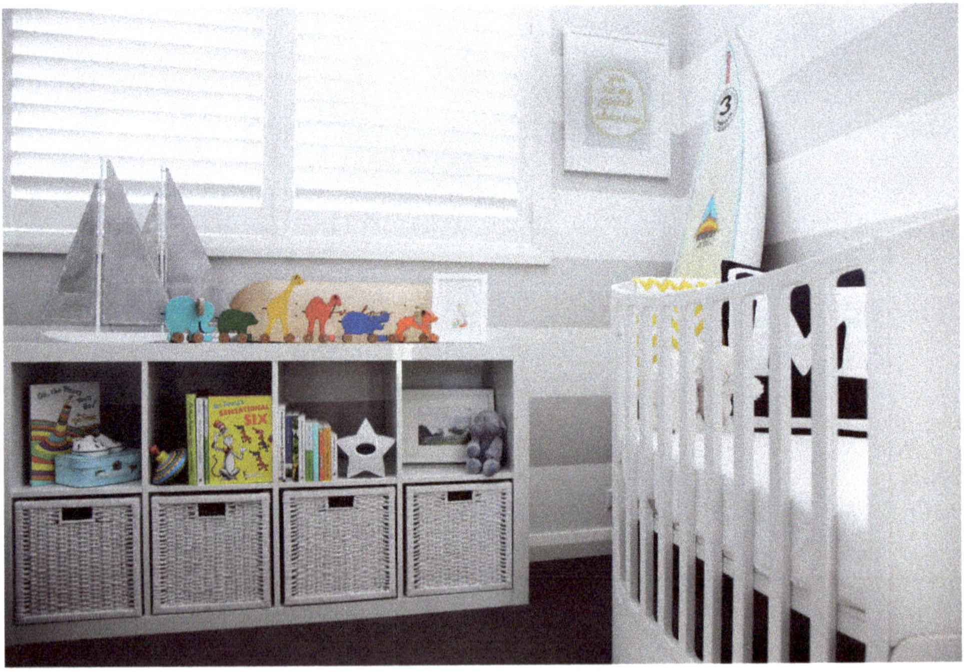
SENSATIONAL
SIX

Leo's Nursery

This room belongs to my youngest son! When I was pregnant with Leo, I was quite sure that this was going to be my last baby. Because of that, I was keen to create a room that was really different to Hugh and Charles' rooms. I had used blues and reds with both of their nurseries and had recently created a shared space for them that was white, black and orange! So, I welcomed the opportunity to create a soft, serene and sophisticated space.

After working with lots of 'traditional' spaces (pink for girls and blue or red for boys) I was so excited to be my own client when I was expecting Leo! I was keen to create a calm and soft space with plenty of white combined with lots of texture.

There were quite a few elements that I chose before we knew if Leo was going to be a boy or a girl. I always knew that I wanted to add copper touches to the space, but I'd thought that if I had a girl I would include coral as a colour to make the details pop. For a boy, I had thought that adding heavier, more masculine textures like leather and timber would make the space a little more suited for a boy. I actually love that it's a soft space that could easily be quite feminine – it really appeals to my tastes (and given that I am the person who spends the most time in this room outside of Leo, it's important to keep me happy!) – but with the use of those more masculine textures it is still the ideal room for a baby boy.

When it came to purchasing the pieces in the room, I started over. I'd used the so many of my first son's pieces in my second son's room, and they were starting to look a little tired! I'd also moved the older two boys into a 'big boys' room together and sold quite a few of their baby pieces. Without a cot, change table or chair, I was working with a blank space.

I had coveted the beautiful Incy Interiors cot for years, and I was also keen to use a dresser with a change mat rather than a traditional change table in order to maximize space. The Empire Rocker was my absolute must-have though and although it was a splurge, it has been worth every penny.

When it came to accessories and little extra bits and pieces I looked for small, unique handmade pieces from makers that I found locally and online, as well as a few additional items that were sourced from our family farm – like the wooden toy box that I added wheels to, and the large timber stump that serves as a side table.

There is a story behind every piece in Leo's room, and it's those little stories that make the space so special. The little 'lion sleeps tonight' banner by Stitch & Shadow was made because this is a song that I sing to Leo before bed each night...after all; he is our little Leo the lion cub! The feather print was made by Piccolo Studio and Brooke provided me with a number of colour options – I fell in love with the watercolour version. We recently celebrated Leo's first birthday and Brooke created invites and a few accessories for the party as well which was really special for me. These items made use of both natural colours and textures so they were the perfect addition to the space. I really encourage using smaller makers as opposed to products that are sold en masse. Not only are you supporting a small business, but you are also guaranteed to create a space that is unique and exceptionally yours.

I absolutely adore Leo's room. Not only is it the tranquil, calm sanctuary that I was hoping for, but already as he begins to grow I am finding that the simple scheme lends itself to so many other options. I will have great fun adding details as he gets older.

There is a lot of white in this space, and it's easy for a room to feel cold with lots of white. By adding loads of texture - timber, leather, fabric - in addition to copper pieces, the room came to life.

I really splashed out with a gorgeous feeding chair in Leo's room and all I could think afterwards was, 'why, oh why, didn't I do that earlier!' Never underestimate the true comfort of a quality feeding chair!

*L*eather is a wonderful way to soften a space. I took a simple Ikea dresser and made it look really luxe by adding leather handles and the sweet leather bookend was the perfect colour!

I added lots of little pieces of 'nature' into Leo's room without it being obvious. References to lions (Leo, of course) in addition to feathers, timber and repurposing a few jungle animals with a spray of copper paint.

Isabella's Nursery

This room was such fun! At the same time, I designed Isabella's big brother's room and this room was actually intended to be a gender neutral space. We went for a colourful and fun design and intially the space had beige walls (not an ideal backdrop for what I'd planned). To lift the room, we painted them a beautiful blue.

Like so many of my clients, Isabella's parents wanted a gender neutral space. There are lots of reasons for this and many of them make perfect sense – sometimes the parents choose to keep gender a surprise until baby arrives, yet they are still keen to set up a room. Other times, the parents might know the sex of their baby, but want to keep it a secret from family or friends. Gender neutral nurseries are beautiful, and even though you can sometimes have a little more fun when you go down a definite path, keeping things simple and for any gender is certainly practical.

The one thing that people need to remember when they start out neutral though is this: you can't control what other people buy for you and your baby! You also can't stop your baby growing and, naturally, having their interests take their possessions in a particular direction! Like it or not, girls' rooms will end up with an abundance of pink and purple bits and boys' rooms tend to gather a significant amount of red (with some blue, yellow and orange in between). So, when I create a truly gender neutral design, I keep that in mind. Will the room still look tasteful and beautiful when it's filled with 'kid stuff'?

For a lot of people, gender neutral means grey or beige, so it was lovely to speak to Isabella's parents and have their brief be bright and colourful! The family home was an old Victorian that had recently been renovated and their style was very modern. This meant that we had huge high ceilings, a large space and picture rails to contend with. Usually, this is wonderful, but it can pose some challenges when you are dealing with modern pieces, which tend to be smaller and sleeker.

We also needed to make use of Isabella's big brother's cot, which had been handed down to her and was quite traditional in style. We had the luxury of purchasing some fun new accessories though, including a fabulous egg chair (which unfortunately hadn't arrived when these images were taken!) I used an egg chair as a feeding chair for my second baby and it was great. Previously, we had used it in another room of the house (and now it's back in the lounge!) and they're practical, comfortable and very stylish options.

The other client must-have was a tree decal. We needed to work within the high skirting boards and the picture rail and I was keen to choose something that was a little bit delicate, just on the off chance that Isabella did turn out to be a girl! Because of those beautiful high ceilings, we also needed to ensure that the decal was the perfect scale – too small and it would look cheap and get a little lost, and too big and we'd hit those beautiful architectural features. I love the design we went with and it was absolutely ideal for the space. What made it even more special was another of my favourite details from this room...that beautiful egg shell blue wall! The paint was the perfect shade and it really complimented all the bright pieces that we'd added to the space – such a fresh colour!

Isabella's parents were thrilled with the final result, and loved that they had a special room ready to bring their little girl home to. I really enjoyed this project, as there were so many fun items that worked perfectly with the scheme.

𝒜 baby's room doesn't need to be full of 'things' to be beautiful - a few keys items brought together in a cohesive way is all it takes to make a space special.

𝒟lue and yellow are considered to be traditional 'boy' colours, which is crazy. This room shows that, really, there is no such thing as a masculine scheme. Anything goes with colour!

Oscar's Nursery

Originally I created two design boards for this little man, as his parents had decided to leave it a surprise as to whether he would be a boy or a girl! The idea was to add a pretty musk pink to the mix if he was a girl, but otherwise go with navy and a soft blue for a boy... which obviously Oscar turned out to be!

I love the little elements of shine and sparkle in this space. It creates such a magical and whimsical feel to the otherwise simple design.

When Oscar's parents contacted me, they had no idea whether they were having a boy or a girl. So, they were keen to create a room that would be easy to transform from gender neutral to 'boy' or 'girl' as soon as their baby arrived. To do this, I created two design boards for them with an identical base and swapped out a few of the key items so that there was a pink version, and a blue one.

'Catch A Falling Star' was a favourite childhood song of Oscar's mum, so it was piece of information that set the theme for the space. Originally, the clients had asked for a grey base, but when they talked about previous design boards that I'd created and they'd loved, I noticed that many of them incorporated silver. So, when I presented silver and grey, they loved it.

The star feature wall actually consists of many, many, many decals! It looks like wallpaper, doesn't it? We can credit Oscar's dad for that skilled (and detailed work!) I am not sure he was happy with me when I suggested it, but he did an amazing job of placing each decal on the wall. They were millimetre perfect and we all loved the end result. It appears to be really striking wallpaper, but by using decals you cannot only easily remove them when you tire of them, you can also create a really unique feature wall.

The clients were keen to use an egg chair as a feeding chair (you can read in the section on Isabella's Nursery from page 54 as to why they make such a great choice!) – selecting one in grey meant that it matched the scheme of the room perfectly, but it will also look great elsewhere in the house when Oscar doesn't need it anymore.

The beautiful cradle in the room was also a must have. It had previously been used by Oscar's big brother and the client was looking forward to using it again. Oscar's big brother was sleeping in a white cot when Oscar arrived and this would also be passed down for Oscar to use, so I needed to take that into consideration when designing the space and colour scheme as well.

Outside of those pieces though, we had a lot of scope to add new items to the room. Many of the items were found from special makers and then others, like the Kewpie Doll light, arrived from overseas. The gorgeous felt gumball rug, which is so popular right now, was a purchase that will last the test of time and will also look lovely in other rooms in the home.

The greatest challenge in this room was light...or lack thereof! The space only had one light source and that was a teeny window on one wall. It was important to keep the colours light and bright so that the room didn't feel too dark or closed in.

I love Oscar's space, it's such a lovely, light room with so many magical pieces. The clients tell me they adore it too, and find it to be a beautifully serene room – one that they all enjoy spending time in. You can't ask for more than that, can you?

This soft and gentle space is perfect for a new baby, and that little addition of sparkle throughout creates a magical feeling that the family will remember forever.

I love shelves that allow you to face books out (and so do the kids!) Being able to choose a book is easier, and the covers create a rotating piece of art!

𝒜 few of the items from this room (the rug, cushion, pouffe, artwork, mobile) are also available in a pink version - perfect just in case Oscar had turned out to be a girl!

Cooper's Nursery

There were some early challenges with Cooper's room. It was a very small space and one wall was completely dominated by a mirrored wardrobe. Cooper's parents wanted to incorporate a very slight safari theme in the room but they also needed it to be gender neutral (as Cooper's gender was a surprise until he arrived) and we needed to keep the space light and bright.

Cooper was the first child of two of my lovely clients (and it just so happens that he is also my beautiful nephew!) They were so excited to create a room for their baby. One of the great bonuses of first time parents (along with their lovely enthusiasm for all things baby!) is that usually they are in a position to purchase new items.

The reason purchasing new is often handy is that you can really create the right space with the items that you buy. In this instance, we were dealing with a teeny, tiny room and I can only imagine the trouble we would have been in had we had further restrictions with large pieces of furniture! The furniture we got fit the space perfectly and gave these first time parents the peace of mind they needed to be sure they had everything they would need.

Other than space, we also had restrictions in that we couldn't do anything permanent to the walls – no wallpaper and no painting. This comes up every now and then – many people rent and are scared to do anything special in their home because they can't paint or wallpaper. However I encourage people not to worry about things like this. Between removable wall decals and 3M strips that can hang almost any art without issue, you have no excuses any more!

We chose to use a gorgeous initial decal over the cot and showcase it with some pretty bunting. Not only did this add a focal point to the room, but the bunting also added some much needed colour and it also helped reinforce the colour scheme that we'd chosen. I also made use of another decal to introduce the 'modern safari' theme that the clients were after. The simple white giraffe decal found a home on the mirrored wardrobe doors and created a little bit of fun and whimsy in the space.

Artwork, soft toys and selected wooden toys also added to the safari theme and this is a great example of how you can create a theme without going bananas...no pun intended! So many people would think of a safari or jungle theme of being greens and browns, a big tree on the wall and loads of stuffed animals. You don't always need to be so literal and sometimes less is much more.

Less is more was a bit of a mantra in this space and the client was so happy with the practicalities as well as the pretties. The little suitcases on the drawers offered a cute way to display goodies...but also served a double purpose as home to some of Cooper's more precious items. The cloud mobile is beautiful and, although the colours match the space and the cloud is a nod to the outdoors and the jungle, I was also conscious that we needed to not clutter the line of sight with unnecessary things.

Cooper's parents wanted a space that was practical, light, bright and fresh, and they were also keen to include safari animals. It's always so nice to hear that I've delivered on brief and then some.

Cooper's room is small, but it still required all the essentials. By playing with light and the reflection of the large wardrobe across one wall, we were able to make the space feel much bigger than it is.

This gallery wall was really special to the clients - every single piece had special meaning to the family, to Cooper and to the theme of the room.

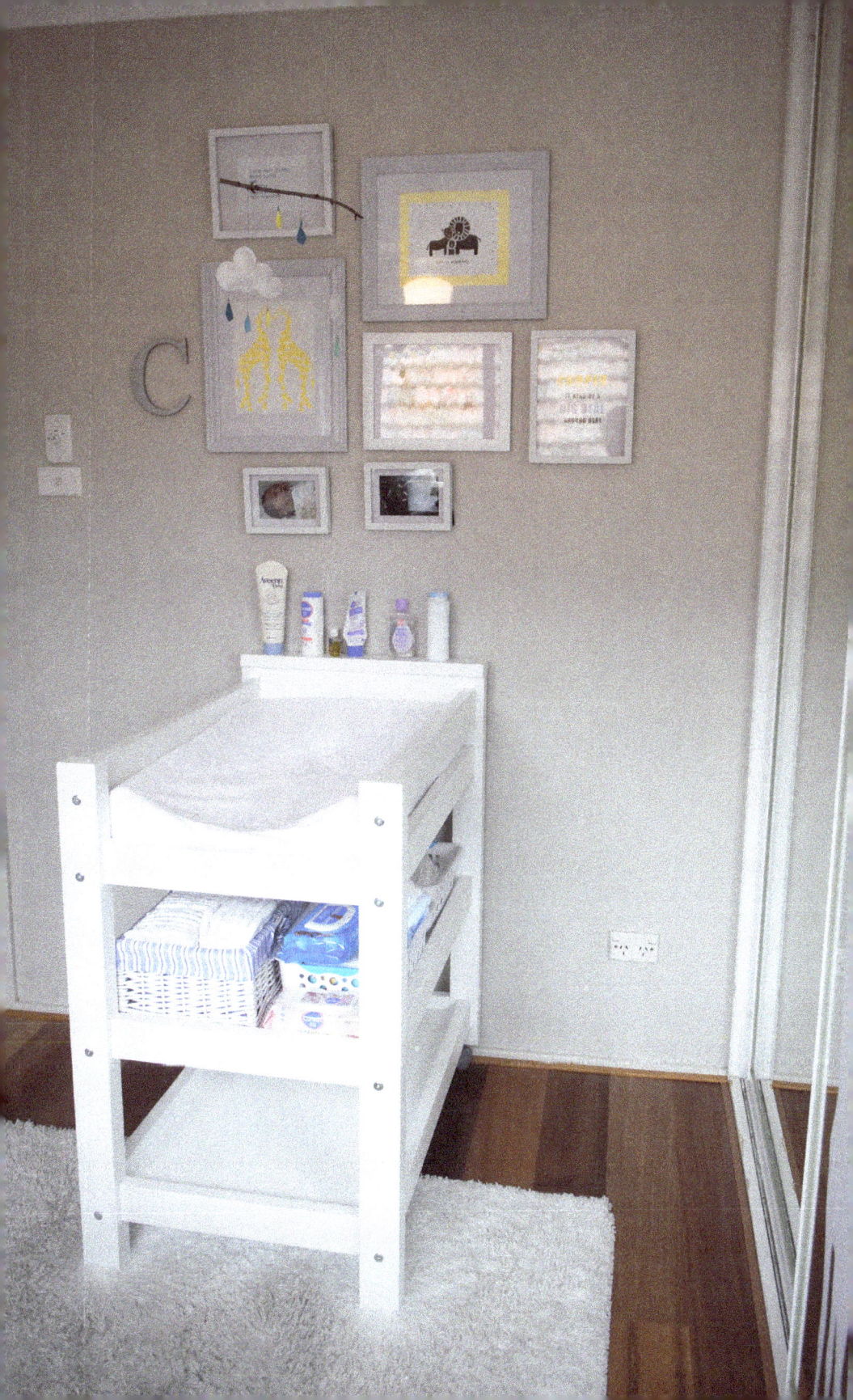

Patrick's Nursery

Bright, fun and full of print and colour - that was the brief for this little boy's space. With the rest of the house being contemporary and new, I was keen to include the same love of modern pieces in to Patrick's room. At the same time, I wanted to ensure that the larger, more expensive items were timeless enough to last the distance. Patrick's mother works in design so each piece is a bit of a nod to the things she loves.

Patrick's parents had just moved in to a new home when they contacted me about his room, and they were keen to extend their existing style in to his space. That meant a contemporary space with bold shapes and bright colours.

Patrick's mother is a graphic designer and she absolutely adores pattern, print and colour so I knew that I could have a little fun with some of the pieces and she would appreciate them. She'd also purchased a large print for the room that she was keen to use, so we worked around this with the design.

The clients had already purchased a cot and change table, and Patrick's grandmother had gifted them the beautiful butterfly mobile, so we had a great start. There are always challenges with new homes though. They tend to lack the character and warmth that you find in an older house and it's really, really easy (especially when you've got lots of new furniture pieces) to have it look like a show home. So, perhaps our only challenge when working with this space was injecting a little love, warmth and spirit in to the room. I really wanted the nursery to feel instantly warm and instantly loved.

The other thing that I really needed to keep in mind was the location of the home. Patrick's family live in regional New South Wales and they were keen to look at some of the larger items in person – particularly the feeding chair. Patrick's mother wanted to make sure that she could sit on the chair before purchasing it (which is a great idea, especially if you are buying a chair that is not purpose built for feeding!) This meant that I needed to provide options from nearby stores to allow her the ability to do this.

I think my favourite item in the room is that awesome collection of block prints. I'd seen them when looking for artwork for another client and as soon as we started talking print and pattern I knew they'd would be perfect for the space. What is really great is that the client will be able to pick colours and prints from that art as time goes on, and completely change the look of the room if they choose to. It's great fun and artwork like this offers lots of scope. The fun of the patterns, and the depth and warmth of the timber base also added to that friendly feeling we were trying to create.

A lot of people are afraid of prints – or don't like them much – but I think they're fabulous and you can have great fun with them. Visually, they're great for young children as well and as your child gets older you can enjoy all sorts of discussion about art, colour and design.

The client wanted soft yellows and whites as the base colours and they were keen to create a space that was crisp, modern and bright. The addition of items like the lamp, the gorgeous Caitlin Wilson cushions and the Anna Castelli Ferrieri Componibili side table offered the elements with that on-trend feel that they were after. All of these items will work equally well in another room of the house if Patrick's parents move things around later on – an investment well made!

This room uses the same colours as Marley's room (back on page 36) and yet both rooms feel completely different. Colour is important, but there is so much more to making a room look and feel a certain way.

Patrick's mum is a graphic designer so I was keen to add lots of graphic elements to the space, but in a very subtle way, as I knew she would appreciate the detail.

Brydie's Nursery

This was initially another gender neutral space (so many people like their surprises!) and I was convinced that this little one was going to be a boy! Shows how much I know. I needed to make use of a few pieces of existing furniture (such as the rocking chair, which was a family heirloom) and I also was asked to incorporate elephants - a theme that came about from a single gift.

Brydie was my client's first baby and so whilst the parents were in a position to buy their must-haves new, they'd also inherited a special item that they wanted included. This is something that happens a lot and second-hand pieces are fabulous, but sometimes they can restrict your design choices a little. Because the feeding chair and the cot were slightly different timbers and stains, I initially recommended stripping the chair back and painting it white. However, the chair had once belonged to the client's grandmother and was a really sentimental piece, so they were keen to keep it as is. We re-covered it in a lovely, simple fabric to suit the new space and the combinations actually create a warm and eclectic feel.

Outside of the large items, the only other baby item in the space, when I first spoke to the clients, was a little toy elephant. Brydie's mother had received it as a baby shower gift and she just loved it, so she thought perhaps elephants might have been a nice theme or starting point for the room. Brydie's gender was to be a surprise though and she hadn't arrived when I started working on the nursery...so a gender neutral room it was to be! Interestingly, Brydie's mother and I both 'felt' that a boy was on the way, and we definitely skewed some choices towards teal and green because of that. It certainly shows how wrong you can be - but it also shows that those traditional 'boy' colours can look just as pretty in a little girl's space!

The one major requirement that the clients were keen for was a lovely big rug. The gorgeous one we selected was from Freedom Furniture and it is so soft it's ridiculous. I know that Brydie and her parents will get plenty of floor time thanks to that rug, and the light colour helped lift the room given it had dark wall-to-wall carpet.

The rug helped keep the space quite neutral and I also adored the feature wall that we created. It was a beautiful, calming paint colour and the decals were actually a breeze to apply. It immediately created a warmer, softer feel in the space and as Brydie grows she will be able to imagine her elephants coming through the trees!

On the topic of elephants though, choosing a theme like this was definitely an example of where things can get crazy quickly! When family and friends knew that the nursery was an elephant theme, they went a little mad. Brydie's mother was a little inundated with elephant items! Luckily, I try to keep things simple and subtle and we'd only chosen four elephant items to begin with, but I imagine the elephant toys and prints will continue to arrive as Brydie gets older.

Themes aside, I think Brydie's parents were happier than almost any of my clients have been because there was so much sentimentality associated with every item in this space. All of the pieces had special meaning - right down to the love heart print on the wall (custom made to include words from the song that the clients first danced to as a married couple at their wedding) and the elephant decal has Brydie's name printed all over it. Beautiful!

$\mathcal{W}$e needed to incorporate quite a few sentimental and existing elements into Brydie's nursery which created a challenge, but also resulted in her parents adoring the space!

Brydie's mum was convinced Brydie was going to be a boy (and I was too) so there is an element of blue in the space! I'm sure a year from now we won't recognise this space with the pink-ification that will occur.

Alec's Nursery

The brief for Alec's space was to create a coastal inspired nursery. Alec's mum wanted texture, as well as a subtle seaside and travel theme and she was also keen for me to keep the general feel of the space soft and gentle.

This room proves that you can create a well-loved, vintage vibe by using plenty of brand new items. You just need to know where to find them!

Alec's family live in a small coastal town and you can actually spot the ocean from his bedroom window (the lucky little man!) so it was no surprise when his parents told me they were keen for a coastal inspired space. I wanted to create a soft and gentle room, so rather than going down the 'beach' track when it came to theming the room, I offered more a nautical theme with a with a subtle seaside and travel element, and lots of texture.

This room is a great example of how you can create a warm and almost vintage feel with brand new items. The only item that the clients already had when they spoke with me was their lovely cot. It was actually a hand-me-down from a friend and they'd also been offered another cot from a friend, but it was a really modern design. The only items that the clients were keen for was a great chair and they'd also thought about using a grass cloth wallpaper. In the end, the wallpaper was a little too expensive and I felt that we could add texture in many other ways – which we certainly did.

One of the tricks to remember when decorating a children's space is that you don't always have to use 'baby décor'. So many of the items in this room were found in vintage inspired stores, or general homewares stores and they look absolutely perfect in the room. Many of the little details – the globe, the bookends, the shoes, the atlas and the map on the wall were all brand new purchases and some of them were from Typo which is technically a stationary store! The compass did belong to Alec's grandfather though, so we still managed to include some sentimental items in the mix.

Alec's room is a fabulous way of showing how well texture can bring life to a space. Items like the toy chest, side table, book shelves and lamp are all a unique, raw timber or hessian and even the footstool and cushion are from a heavy, thick cotton that adds depth to the room. The throw rugs on the chair and cot also add a feeling of warmth and texture. Incorporating natural materials in to a room is a really easy way to bring it to life and there are lots of ways that you can do it. By choosing items that are lovely to touch (like timber, wool and cotton) you can instantly make people feel at ease.

You might also spot the rug on the floor – a lovely gumball felt rug – and remember that it is the same style of rug that Oscar had in his room (page 60). This is a great way to see how differently the same item can look when styled with different items.

The thing that I really love about this room is that the client actually ended up using every single one of my recommendations! That doesn't always happen, and I can understand why, but it's always so lovely to see everything come together like this. It is really a beautiful space and so great to see my vision come alive in such a perfect way! I am so excited to now be working on Alec's big boy room.

Using texture is an excellent way to add warmth to a space, particularly if the colours you are using (white, grey and blue) can often feel a little cold.

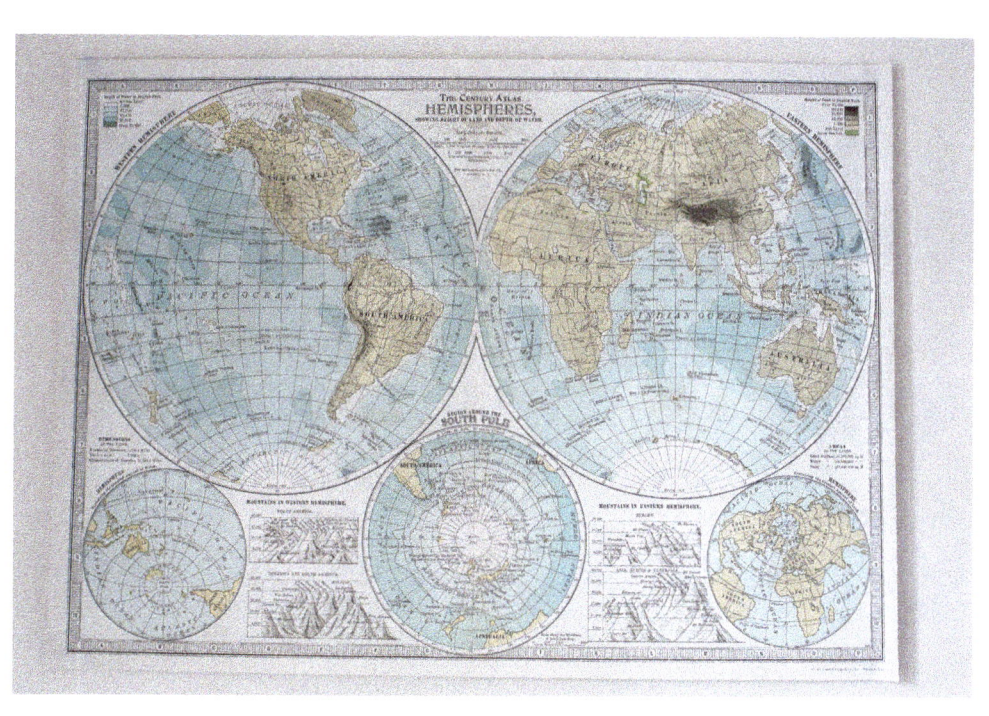

𝓐lec (the lucky thing!) has a sea view from his room, so a nautical theme was ideal. We went with a vintage style to keep it a little different as opposed to going all out with beachy items.

Orla Kiely
creatures
Orla Kiely
numbers
Orla Kiely
colors
Orla Kiely
shapes

Charles' Nursery

Can you believe that this entire space started with a onesie?! Yep, if you have a look at page 116, you will see the inspiration right there. It is proof that a beautiful idea can start in the most unlikely of places. I also had a tight budget with this space, in addition to restrictions that came about from needing to use existing furniture. The end result was a nursery that came together better than I could have hoped.

A lot of people tell me that they have no idea where to begin when it comes to styling a room. I can understand why – sometimes the sheer volume of choice is overwhelming. The thing is, often when I am meeting with a client we come up with a concept for a room from the simplest thing...a favourite colour, a childhood nursery rhyme, a family interest, a toy or blanket that is special. From there, you can build an entire space and fill it with things that have meaning to you and your family.

Charles' room is a classic example of this! He had a onesie that I just loved, so the stripes were scaled and the colour matched to it. I also had a few beautiful books that led to adding a loose travel theme to the room.

The other thing that is important to note about Charles' room is the budget...it was minimal and it's definite proof that you don't have to spend a bomb to achieve a great look. The cot and the change table once belonged to Charles' big brother, Hugh, and the red egg chair once lived in the lounge room! I have a tendency to move items around the house and from room to room quite often and I always encourage others to do the same. Don't ever feel that the items in a room are limited to just that room!

The other cost-saving trick was DIY. I painted the wall myself, made artwork and used Ikea spice racks as book shelves (spray-painted white). Another DIY was the mobile that I created from an old atlas making little globes featuring places that were special to us - where we'd been on our honeymoon, where family members had been born and their home towns.

One of my 'must haves' for this room was a reading nook. I knew that I'd have a busy two-year-old wanting me at feeding time, so really that space was set up for my older son. Having a little area that entertained him during feeding times was fantastic and we looked at a lot of books for those first few months. What was really great was seeing Charles exploring the same space, as he got a little older, and loving it. I would recommend to any second (or third or more) time mother to set up a little reading nook in their baby's room. It will allow a special bonding time with all of your children that is just wonderful.

Charles' room wasn't huge and a lot of people would be nervous about using a bold colour like red in an area like that (especially a baby's room!) but I loved it. With the soft blue, navy and white as accent colours it was actually a very calm room and the white furniture made the whole room feel light and spacious. It's really important to not make assumptions about colour. When you experiment with what you love you might be surprised with the results.

There's a lot said about 'nesting' and the crazy things women do towards the end of their pregnancy. I love to paint walls, but I did those stripes at 36 weeks pregnant which is possibly just a little crazy. In saying that, if you are feeling inspired to do something physical around the house at that stage then, go for it! If I'd waited until he was born it may never have happened...and I did love that wall!

 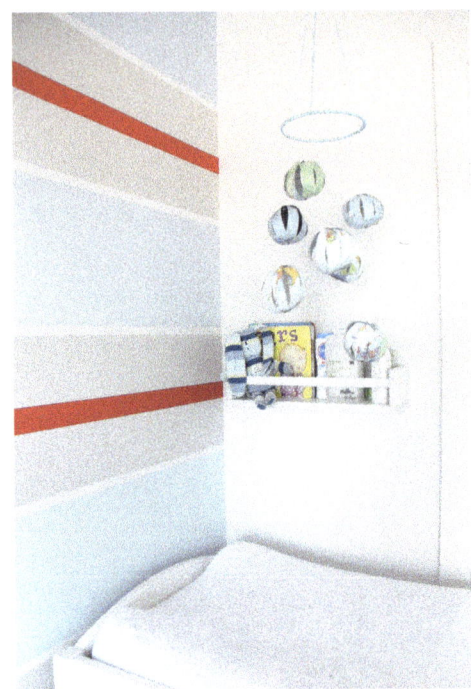

$\mathcal{I}$ made a lot of items in this room (and repurposed a few as well!) Those little bookshelves on the wall above the change table? Spice racks from Ikea sprayed white! The mini globes (above left) were made using an old atlas.

Choosing a theme (like travel) can get cheesey quickly. By choosing just a few elements - books, maps, wooden toys - and then telling the rest of the story with colour, we kept things a little more subtle.

Story's Nursery

Being the mother of three little boys, I had an absolute ball creating this wonderful room fit for a princess! There is no question that girls get the lion's share of pretty items, but at the same time, having an abundance of choice means that can be easy to get it wrong. We chose elegant musk pink and peach shades in this room to embrace the prettiness, whilst still making it timeless and classic.

When I designed Leo's room (page 44) I presented a girl's version and a boy's version of the design board on social media. Story's parents absolutely loved the girl's room ideas and contacted me to help them create a similar soft and girly space for their daughter. They wanted to include some Cinderella touches (in the form of the large artwork above the dresser) and lots of white with touches of pink, gold and texture. They also loved the crisp Hamptons style of décor so the final brief was girly, romantic, sparkly and pretty. What fun!

This is exactly why I love sharing my design boards with people. As you can see from the page to the left, they are full of inspiration and they really capture the look and feel of the space before you do any work or spend a lot of money! Sometimes people don't know what they like until they see it, so a design board is perfect for that as well. Even if you don't want to pay for a professional designer, you can always use this concept yourself to see how things look together in a space – do the styles work side by side or do the colours work well when they're all together?

In this instance, the clients had already purchased the Leander cot, but other than that they were keen to start afresh with other items when I started designing the space. There were a few items that Story's mum had seen that she was hoping to incorporate – the Nursery Works Empire Rocker, a beautiful sheepskin rug and the 'all you need is kindness and courage' print. In fact, our only real worry was whether or not we would be able to fit everything on her wish list into the room, as it was quite a small space. However, with good planning and working cleverly with the space, we were able to include it all and then some! The final list of large items included a dresser, a cot, a large chair, a side table, a canopy and a wall of forward facing bookshelves...not bad at all!

There are some beautiful features in the room as well – I just want to curl up on some cushions under that dreamy canopy with a good book! So many of the itesm will be perfect for Story in the years to come...even more so if she loves princesses like so many little girls do. It is a space fit for a little Queen! The accents of gold, rose gold and glitter add the perfect amount of sparkle, and the neutral, warm tones of the timber elements offer a softness and texture to the room.

I loved this dream space – it was filled with so many personal favourites of mine! I am looking at new products all the time and there really are so many beautiful items out there. The other thing that I loved about this space was the fact that it really reinforced how successful online design can be. I live in central Victoria and Story's family live on the other side of the country in Western Australia. I've never met the clients in person and yet I was able to create something perfect for them using my e-design model.

The clients were thrilled with the final result. It was exactly what they wanted and they couldn't have been happier. Even better, Story loves her room already too! Her mum tells me that she loves watching the wooden tassles above her bed sway in the breeze...it puts her sleep. That's what I'd call successful room design.

I think every child's room should have a reading nook if there is space. Encouraging your child to have quiet time in their room early on is definitely something that is good for everyone as time goes on.

*T*hose coloured suitcases create such an impact without even trying - a little splash of mint green and turquoise to perfectly compliment the main colour scheme.

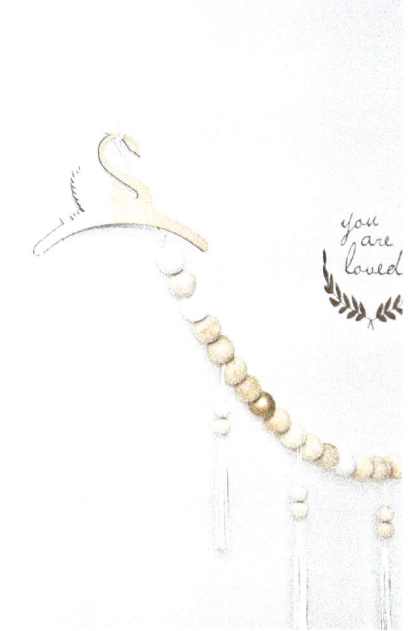

you are
loved

I adore the details in this room...there is something new to see each time you look at the space. Story will have great fun exploring her room as she gets older!

When using a designer...

There are a lot of misconceptions when it comes to hiring a designer. I mean, it's expensive, right? They have super dooper, over the top taste and unrealistic ideas about how to create beautiful rooms, don't they? WRONG!

One of the things that many potential clients assume is that I (or any other designer, for that matter) will specify ridiculously priced items in order to create the room. And I can tell you that any designer worth their salt will not do that!

I am just like any other mum and we are just like any other family. We raise our family of five with my husband's wage and whatever I make from my business on that day/week/month (anyone who has their own business will understand that one!) My husband is just like yours - he doesn't understand why on earth I need new cushions or decorative 'knick knacks' of any type. When it comes to decorating my home, I have to do it on a budget (or whatever I can sneak in)!

I have three little boys - there is no way I would specify a $100+ cushion for their room because I know exactly what they're like. In fact, I wouldn't specify one for the lounge room either...because I have three little boys and a messy husband! I believe that most people want to create a beautiful space AND spend as little as possible...even those out there who may have the luxury of larger budgets.

When I created Charles' nursery (opposite), the whole space cost me about $700 (including the cot, but excluding the feeding chair...we owned it and I moved it from the lounge to his room when he was born! The little table and chair were his birthday present, so they're not included in the price either).

Hugh's room (below) cost even less as most of it was DIY. I was desperate for a tree wall decal, but I couldn't justify paying the price of having one made to measure (of course I had a particular tree in mind!) So, I took a grey lead pencil and sketched it right onto the wall. From there, I painted the tree using regular, old fashioned wall paint. Yes, it took some work, but it cost next to nothing!

When it comes to designing a room for a client, I really try to keep the items recommended well within the client's budget. There are fabulous websites - like Etsy - that help you find individual pieces for very little. I do think it is lovely to splurge on one design item if you can though - it will last a long time and it really something special for your child.

Don't get me wrong, I can spend with best of them (and I will if you want me to!) but you're not to be scared about what a designer may recommend. It's their job to know where to find all the best, more unique items...at the best price too! So don't be afraid to give a designer a go.

The perfect shelfie

If you spend any time on social media these days, it's hard to avoid the 'shelfie' - it's the interior enthusiasts version of the 'selfie' and it can be just as in your face as it sounds! It can be quite frustrating to see people's photos that show randomly shoved together items that just look perfect and then when you try to do the same it looks like a bunch of junk all bundled on a shelf!

When you are the parent of a baby, you only have about eight or nine months before those items are being pulled to the floor (you might get longer with higher shelves!) so enjoy the pretty while you can. Here are some tips to make your shelves look just as pretty as the special things on them:

1. Vary heights. Make sure you create some height balance when it comes to items in groups - if you have items of different heights, try up-down-up-again to keep it interesting.

2. Less is more. You don't need to jam every single item you own on a shelf. Leaving strategically open spaces can make just as big a statement!

3. Use books as a base. Group books by colour, recover mismatched books with decorative paper or, if you have a favourite, place it front and centre with the cover facing the room. Use little items that you love as bookends to a stacked pile. Arrange and rearrange until you find a combo that you love. Don't be afraid to stack vertically and horizontally.

4. Add the unexpected. A plant, a special toy, their first pair of shoes...book shelves don't just need to be the home of books.

5. Make it your own. It's tempting to copy from someone else's Instagram or Pinterest but this is a place that it really should mean something to you more than anyone else! Your dad's old bear, your shoes, the first 'something' that was purchased when you knew you were expecting. That's what makes it all special.

6. Keep it fresh. The perfect shelf arrangement should be a constant work in progress, not a dust-gathering diorama! Don't be afraid to add, subtract or just move things around as baby grows.

7. Display a collection. If you've got a few of one type of item, group them by colour, size or type to create a pretty assortment rather than having things scattered everywhere.

In Leo's room (opposite), I wanted to keep with the colour scheme of tan, bronze and white/cream - not an easy task when you are dealing with babies toys and accessories! By keeping with soft greys and blues for many of the toys that are on display, I also looked for some of my favourite items in a colour that matched my theme. The suitcases (perfect for storage), the slinky, the sqwish, the blocks and the leather bookend all come in other colours as well. Adding unexpected items in the palette - like the plants - make the scene fresh.

Creating a gallery

Another fabulous way to add instant colour and life to a room is by creating a photo gallery or mini art installation. A lot of people are scared at the thought of having to hang pictures in perfect symmetry but that's the beauty of this trend - it doesn't have to be perfect! Even better, with all these clever products on hand these days (like those brilliant, removable 3M strips) you can make as many mistakes as you like in trying to get it right. To help you along though, here are a few ideas that may help:

1. Find the right wall. Make sure you've got enough space to hang your images without overwhelming the room (or the people looking at the wall).

2. Select your images. This can be an overwhelming process, but also loads of fun! Choose a theme - like a colour scheme - that will link them together and scour websites and online stores like Etsy to put together a little collection. You may like to include family images or leave space for images of baby as he or she grows as well. When it comes time to buy or print them, mix up the sizes and consider the frame they are going into beforehand (sometimes that is easier than finding a frame to suit after the fact)!

3. Mix up your frames. Your frames don't have to be all exactly the same type and size (although that can look pretty great too). Combine a variety of frame styles and sizes and bring them together by having them all the one colour. In saying that, a mix of colours can add interest and sometimes it's great to frame a piece of art to suit the work...as opposed to just popping it in any frame!

4. Lay it out. Take all your framed pieces and lay them out on the floor. Move them around until you are happy with the mix. This will allow you to space everything out before you go to the trouble of getting them up on the wall! A great starting point is to put your largest image in the centre and build from there.

5. Stay original. There are often 'designs' of choice that become the trend of the moment. There's nothing wrong with jumping on board what's in fashion if you really love it, but it will mean so much more in the long run if you go with a personal choice that means something to you or your family.

6. Take your time. Curating your own personal art gallery shouldn't be done in a day. Spend some time thinking about what you want and looking at different sources and enjoy the process. Find images and words that tug at your heartstrings and make you feel good. They will be the ones that calm you down after that bundle of joy has just spent the last hour crying instead of sleeping!

The wall in Victoria's room (opposite) that we chose to use as a gallery wall included a heating vent. By using white frames, the vent simply disappeared in amongst the artwork! Don't let tricky spaces put you off doing something creative - there is usually always a way around it.

Don't forget to have fun!

Remember, that when it comes down to it all, the most important thing is that beautiful new baby in your arms. That baby who just wants your cuddles and your warmth...and not much else! Creating a beautiful space in any room of your home should be filled with fun and delight, so keep it all in perspective.
If it feels like it all seems too hard, then don't do it!

Photography Credits

Cover image from Leo's Nursery (front): Belinda Nihill *(www.nestdesignstudio.com.au)*

Cover image from Victoria's Nursery (rear): Anneke Hill *(www.annekehill.com.au)*

Head shot of Belinda (rear): Kate Monotti *(www.katemonottiphotography.com.au)*

Page 1 (from Story's Nursery): Lauren Scott *(www.tilliefrank.bigcartel.com)*

Page 2 & 4 (from Alec's Nursey): Rainee Lantry *(www.cloudninephotography.net.au)*

Page 5 (from Oscar's Nursey): Belinda Nihill *(www.nestdesignstudio.com.au)*

Page 6 (from Hugo's Nursery): Louise Treacy *(www.louisetreacyphotography.com.au)*

Page 8 (from Victoria's Nursery): Anneke Hill *(www.annekehill.com.au)*

Page 9 (from Marley's Nursery): Anneke Hill *(www.annekehill.com.au)*

Page 10 (from Leo's Nursery): Belinda Nihill *(www.nestdesignstudio.com.au)*

Page 11 (from Oscar's Nursery): Belinda Nihill *(www.nestdesignstudio.com.au)*

Pages 12-19: Lisa Nankervis *(www.lisanankervis.com)*

Pages 20-27: Anneke Hill *(www.annekehill.com.au)*

Pages 28-35: Louise Treacy *(www.louisetreacyphotography.com.au)*

Pages 36-42: Anneke Hill *(www.annekehill.com.au)*

Pages 44-53: Belinda Nihill *(www.nestdesignstudio.com.au)*

Pages 54-59: Belinda Nihill *(www.nestdesignstudio.com.au)*

Pages 60-67: Belinda Nihill *(www.nestdesignstudio.com.au)*

Pages 68-75: Chantelle Bliss *(www.foreverblissphotography.com.au)*

Pages 76-81: Peter Charlewroth *(www.petercharlesworth.net)*

Pages 82-87: Lisa Nankervis *(www.lisanankervis.com)*

Pages 88-97: Rainee Lantry *(www.cloudninephotography.net.au)*

Pages 98-105: Belinda Nihill *(www.nestdesignstudio.com.au)*

Pages 106-115: Lauren Scott *(www.tilliefrank.bigcartel.com)*

Page 116 (from Charles' Nursery): Belinda Nihill *(www.nestdesignstudio.com.au)*

Page 117 (from Hugh's Nursery): Lisa Nankervis *(www.lisanankervis.com)*

Page 119 (from Leo's Nursery): Belinda Nihill *(www.nestdesignstudio.com.au)*

Page 120 (from Victoria's Nursery): Anneke Hill *(www.annekehill.com.au)*

Page 122 (from Leo's Nursery): Belinda Nihill *(www.nestdesignstudio.com.au)*

Page 124: Elisa Herdman *(www.littlesolesphotography.com.au)*

Page 125: Matthew Nihill

Acknowledgements

Running a business with kids underfoot is certainly a challenging task – even if those kids do offer loads of inspiration!

I'd love to thank my parents for those times when I've really needed a babysitter (and a hug); my husband for embracing the crazy and believing that I can do anything and my friends for all their therapy...I mean support! I've also found a beautiful network of likeminded friends through the online community and they have been such an inspiration and wonderful little 'village' for me over the years - you guys are awesome.

Thanks also to Mel, for her editing skills; and to Amy, for telling me I should put everything together in a book and then pushing me to make it happen.

And, to fat coke and cake – thanks for getting me through the days when the nights prior were sleepless!

About the author

Belinda Nihill found a passion for Interior Design in her early teens when her parents gave her creative license to paint and decorate her bedroom. Long gone now, that sky blue sponged wall with sunflower border details (hey, it was the 1990s after all) is still etched in her mind!

Following 15 years of study and work in the interior design industry, Bel is right back where she started – designing bedrooms!

Soon after discovering her first child was on the way, Belinda was helping a client choose colours for their toddler's bedroom and she realised that this was an area that she would really enjoy specialising in. From that moment on, she started filing away ideas for her own baby's nursery and, as it turned out, many other babies too!

Bel's business, Nest Design Studio, has grown over the years with her work being showcased in magazines and websites from all over the world. Bel says that she absolutely loves working with parents to help them design a room for their little one – a place their child can dream, play and grow. She understands that clients want a room that looks good, but is also very functional – and she speaks from experience. With three little men in her home, she knows kids can make a well organised room look like a disaster zone in minutes!

In 2015, Bel was a finalist in the presigious 'Australian House & Garden Top 50 Rooms' awards.

To find out more about Bel and her business or to contact her for your own design, visit www.nestdesignstudio.com.au or, see more of what she does on instagram (@nestdesignstudio) or facebook (@nestinteriordesign)

www.ingramcontent.com/pod-product-compliance
Lightning Source LLC
Chambersburg PA
CBHW040335300426
44113CB00021B/2754